Bible Highlighting Guide

A BIBLE STUDY COMPANION FROM
THE DAILY GRACE CO.

STEFANIE BOYLES

Contents

All Scripture is inspired by God and is profitable for teaching, for rebuking, for correcting, for training in righteousness, so that the man of God may be complete, equipped for every good work.

2 TIMOTHY 3:16-17

TO BIBLE HIGHLIGHTING

The Bible is the Word of God. We believe that all of Scripture is breathed out by God and is profitable (2 Timothy 3:16-17). We believe it is how God speaks to us. We need the Bible. It is nourishment to our souls. It sustains us in our walk with the Lord. It shows us His glory and reveals His mind and will for our lives. It changes us as it grows us into Christlikeness. It makes us wise, and it brings true joy. This is why God's people strive to read and study His Word. We press into its riches because it is how we know God.

Yet, we can feel like there are many barriers to our study of Scripture. We struggle to follow through with our Bible reading plans. Sometimes, we are tempted to think that only the New Testament is relevant. Or perhaps we wrestle with a lack of desire for God and His Word from time to time. Or maybe we think the only way to have meaningful time in the Word is in the quiet, early morning hours with our journal and highlighters at hand. If our life season does not allow this, then we may be tempted to forego any time in the Word.

We need God's Word in every season of life. And the truth is, we need God's help. Before we approach the Word of God, we intentionally place ourselves in a posture of humility in prayer. We ask the Lord to open our eyes so we may behold wondrous things out of His law (Psalm 119:18). We ask the Holy Spirit to help us before, during, and after our time in the Word. We believe that we need the whole Bible, both the Old Testament and the New Testament. We remind ourselves that the goal is more of God, not a perfect quiet time atmosphere. And we do not give up.

STUDYING INDUCTIVELY

We press in, and we try our best to figure out a Bible study method that works for us. One accessible method for all of us to consider is the inductive method. This is a fruitful approach because it begins by regarding the Word of God alone as the principal source of truth. This approach invites us to engage the text directly before considering biblical insight from other reputable sources, like commentaries and sermons. We begin by observing the text with the goal of comprehension. This may seem simple because most people have mastered some level of reading comprehension by early adulthood. However, accurate comprehension of the text takes effort and skill.

STUDYING TO COMPREHEND

The glorious truth is that a person can study the Bible for hours every single day for the rest of his or her life and still fail to exhaust the riches found in the Word. The Bible is the very words of God. The Holy Spirit authored it through the use of about forty writers over a period of 1,500 years. Every passage is God-breathed and tells the story of redemption. It is cohesive. It is unchanging. It is eternal. It is alive and active. And it is applicable for every season of life. But we need the Spirit's help as we study His Word. It is through our study of the Word that the Holy Spirit transforms our minds and thus our lives. The first step of comprehension in our study is crucial. Without accurate comprehension of the text, we cannot expect to arrive at the correct interpretation and appropriate application.

WHY BIBLE HIGHLIGHTING?

Bible highlighting is a helpful tool in this process of observing the text. There are many other systems available — use of specific symbols, color pencils, etc. Some methods are incredibly intricate. This guide is to offer you an overview of a few simple yet effective systems of using highlighters in your Bible study. It takes effort and discipline to develop your observation and comprehension muscles, but it is a worthy endeavor that will help you faithfully and fruitfully run this race of faith.

The goal is not a beautifully marked up Bible. The goal is to be captivated by the beauty of the gospel through the faithful study of the Word of God. The hope is not behavior modification but a transformed mind and heart in response to the truth of God's Word. The goal is to know God and make Him known in this world. Bible highlighters can be a means to facilitate deep and intentional Bible study to achieve these worthy goals.

Are you ready to know

God through the

study of His Word?

Are you ready to be

transformed?

The Story of Scripture

CREATION ⟶ FALL ⟶ REDEMPTION ⟶ RESTORATION

Though comprised of 66 books, the Bible tells one, cohesive story. This is often referred to as the metanarrative of Scripture. This is the story of redemption, and every passage of Scripture fits into this unified narrative. This big picture of Scripture can be best understood through four plot movements: creation, fall, redemption, and restoration (consummation). Understanding these different aspects of the greater narrative helps us understand who God is, how He works, and His plan of redemption through the ages. Our understanding of the greater narrative can also serve as a guiding theme that illumines all of the other themes found in individual books of the Bible. Remember, the Bible is cohesive. Here is a brief overview of the plot movements that make up the metanarrative of Scripture.

Genesis 1:1 says, "In the beginning God created the heavens and the earth." But before He created the sun, moon, stars, and earth, He existed in perfect unity within Himself. There was perfect love and fellowship in the Trinity among the Father, the Son, and the Holy Spirit. It was out of an overflow of this love that God created everything else. He created man in His image, and He called all that He made "very good" (Genesis 1:31). There was perfect peace on earth because there was the presence of God. God was there, and He walked with Adam and Eve in the garden of Eden. Adam and Eve were told to be "fruitful and multiply" and to have dominion over the earth (Genesis 1:28). They were to worship God by loving Him and obeying this command.

But there was a fallen angel (Satan) who wanted to steal God's glory. He disguised Himself as a serpent and tempted the woman to disobey God. In Genesis 3:1, the serpent said to the woman, "Did God really say, 'You can't eat from any tree in the garden'?" God told them to not eat from one tree in the garden: the tree of the knowledge of good and evil. The serpent was crafty, and in twisting God's words, he caused Eve to doubt God's goodness and abundant provision. Adam and Eve ate the forbidden fruit, and sin entered the world. There was no longer peace on earth. Instead, there was death and brokenness due to sin. Unfortunately, sin would infect every human heart coming after Adam and Eve. God's people were in need of a redeemer to save them.

As soon as sin entered the world, God proclaimed the good news that a redeemer would come and claim victory over the serpent. In Genesis 3:15, God told Satan, "I will put hostility between you and the woman, and between your offspring and her offspring; He will strike your head, and you will strike his heel." This verse is known as the *proto-evangelium*, which means the first gospel. It is the proclamation that God would ultimately claim victory over the serpent, and this victory would be through the person and work of Jesus Christ. On this side of the cross, we know Jesus came, just as He said He would. Being fully God and fully man, He lived the perfect life we could not live, and He died as the perfect sacrifice on behalf of our sins. He then conquered death in His resurrection, and He offers His people reconciliation with God by freely giving us His righteousness. Now, those in Christ, are free from the curse of sin and are spiritually alive now and for all of eternity!

Soon, Jesus will return again. This time, He will come as a righteous judge in unveiled glory. He will gather His people, and He will make a new earth that will be perfect. God's people will have resurrected bodies and live in His presence again. Satan will be defeated once and for all. Those who did not bow to Jesus Christ as Lord and Savior will also be eternally condemned, and those who put their faith in Christ will reign with Him and dwell in His presence forever. This is the glorious future that all of God's people are promised in Christ.

Bible highlighting?

When we approach Bible study, we want to guard against twisting Scripture to serve our needs and desires. Having a deep understanding of the bigger story can help protect the reader from isolating a verse or passage to serve him or herself. When we think of highlighting in the Bible, we often think of marking the verses that stand out to us. If we study with this kind of Bible highlighting approach, we are bound to highlight every verse in the Bible over the course of our lives. We also do not want to foster a habit of going to Scripture for quick fixes or isolating a verse out of context. Though we are free to reserve a highlighter for those specific verses (or maybe the verses you want to commit to memory, for example), it is more helpful to have that as part of a system of highlighting that aids in your observation and comprehension of the text.

Getting Started

First, you need a Bible. We highly recommend choosing a Bible translation that strives for word-for-word translation of the original language. The CSB, ESV and NASB are some of the most reliable word-for-word translations available. These are based on the earliest manuscripts of the Bible in its original language. The KJV and NJKV are also word-for-word translations, but they are based on later manuscripts. Translations such as NLT and The Message are actually paraphrases, which means the author has applied his interpretation of the text in the translation. These should be handled more as commentaries.

Next, grab a set of highlighters that won't bleed through the pages of your Bible. The Daily Grace Company offers a variety of highlighters that do not bleed through or smear, specifically meant for thinner pages. If you do not feel comfortable highlighting and writing in your Bible, copy and paste the text into a word processor, and format it to be double-spaced with extra room in the margin. This is handy when you're planning on spending extended time in a particular chapter or book of the Bible because it leaves room for questions and thoughts that come up during the inductive process.

A Note on Repetitive Reading

It is very difficult to identify key words and themes in a book without repetitive reading. If you are working through a shorter book of the Bible (like Nahum in the Old Testament or 1 John in the New Testament), it is helpful to read the entire book in one sitting, especially the first few times you encounter the book. This will take the average reader about 10-15 minutes. Repetitive reading will help you grasp the key themes in the particular book. Each time you read through the passage, you can have one highlighter in hand and identify that particular category throughout the book. As you read through the text, mark verses that seem obscure. These are verses you can return to for further study. If you are working through a longer book of the Bible, you can apply the same principles by splitting the book up into smaller portions.

This does not have to be daunting. There are many audio Bible apps available free of charge. Although you may not be able to highlight while you are listening, you will be exposing yourself to the text and engaging your different senses. This will help you recognize repeating words and themes and allow you to better understand the overall passage.

READY TO GET STARTED?

| PENS & HIGHLIGHTERS | BIBLE OR DOUBLE SPACED COPY OF THE PASSAGE | FAMILIARIZE YOURSELF WITH THE TEXT BY READING OR LISTENING |

Philippians (continued)

you and now tell you even with ...enemies of the cross of Christ, ...struction, their god is their belly, ...their shame, with minds set on ...our citizenship is in heaven, ...wait a Savior, the Lord Jesus ...transform our lowly body to ...body, by the power that en- ...subject all things to himself ...brothers, whom I love and ...and crown, stand firm thus ...ed.

...gement, and Prayer

...nd I entreat Syntyche to ...nd I ask also, true com- ...men, who have labored ...he gospel together with ...f my fellow workers, ...ook of life.

...vays; again I will say, ...ableness be known ...hand; do not be ...at in everything by ...thanksgiving let ...to God. And the ...all understand- ...your minds in

...s true, whatever ...hatever is pure, ...mmendable, if ...anything wor- ...things. What ...heard and ...and the God

God's Provision

I rejoiced in the Lord greatly that now at length you have revived your concern for me. You were indeed concerned for me, but you had no opportunity. Not that I am speaking of being in need, for I have learned in whatever situation I am to be content. I know how to be brought low, and I know how to abound. In any and every circumstance, I have learned the secret of facing plenty and hunger, abundance and need. I can do all things through him who strengthens me.

Yet it was kind of you to share my trouble. And you Philippians yourselves know that in the beginning of the gospel, when I left Macedonia, no church entered into partnership with me in giving and receiving, except you only. Even in Thessalonica you sent me help for my needs once and again. Not that I seek the gift, but I seek the fruit that increases to your credit. I have received full payment, and more. I am well supplied, having received from Epaphroditus the gifts you sent, a fragrant offering, a sacrifice acceptable and pleasing to God. And my God will supply every need of yours according to his riches in glory in Christ Jesus. To our God and Father be glory forever and ever. Amen.

Final Greetings

Greet every saint in Christ Jesus. The brothers who are with me greet you. All the saints greet you, especially those of Caesar's household.

The grace of the Lord Jesus Christ be with your spirit.

THE LETTER OF PAUL TO THE

COLOSSIANS

For the Introduction to Colossians see page 1057

Greeting

1 Paul, an apostle of Christ Jesus by the will of God, and Timothy our brother,

To the saints and faithful brothers in Christ at Colossae:

Grace to you and peace from God our Father.

Thanksgiving and Prayer

We always thank God, the Father of our Lord Jesus Christ, when we pray for you, since we heard of your faith in Christ Jesus and of the love that you have for all the saints, because of the hope laid up for you in heaven. Of this you have heard before in the word of the truth, the gospel, which has come to you, as indeed in the whole world it is bearing fruit and increasing—as it also does among you, since the day you heard it and understood the grace of God in truth, just as you learned it from Epaphras our beloved fellow servant. He is a faithful minister of Christ on your behalf and has made known to us your love in the Spirit.

And so, from the day we heard, we have not ceased to pray for you, asking that you may be filled with the knowledge of his will in all spiritual wisdom and understanding, so as to walk in a manner worthy of the Lord, fully pleasing to him: bearing fruit in every good work and increasing in the knowledge of God, being strengthened with all power, according to his glorious might, for all endurance and patience with joy; giving thanks to the Father, who has qualified you to share in the inheritance of the saints in light. He has delivered us from the domain of darkness and transferred us to the kingdom of his beloved Son, in whom we have redemption, the forgiveness of sins.

The Preeminence of Christ

He is the image of the invisible God, the firstborn of all creation. For by him all things were created, in heaven and on earth, visible and invisible, whether thrones or dominions or rulers or authorities—all things were created through him and for him. And he is before all things, and in him all things hold together. And he is the head of the body, the church. He is the beginning, the firstborn from the dead, that in everything he might be preeminent. For in him all the fullness of God was pleased to dwell, and through him to reconcile to himself all things, whether on earth or in heaven, making peace by the blood of his cross.

And you, who once were alienated and hostile in mind, doing evil deeds, he has now reconciled in his body of flesh by his death, in order to present you holy and blameless and above reproach before him, if indeed you continue in the faith, stable and steadfast, not shifting from the hope of the gospel that you heard, which has been proclaimed in all creation under heaven, and of which I, Paul, became a minister.

Paul's Ministry to the Church

Now I rejoice in my sufferings for your sake, and in my flesh I am filling up what is lacking in Christ's afflictions for the sake of his body, that is, the church, of which I became a minister according to the stewardship from God that was given to me for you, to make the word of God fully known, the mystery hidden for ages and generations but now revealed to his saints. To them God chose to make known how great among the Gentiles are the riches of the glory of this mystery, which is Christ in you, the hope of glory. Him we proclaim, warning everyone and teaching everyone with all wisdom, that we may present everyone mature in Christ. For this I toil, struggling with all his energy that he powerfully works within me.

2 For I want you to know how great a struggle I have for you and for those at Laodicea and for all who have not seen me face to face, that their hearts may be encouraged, being knit together in love, to reach all the riches of full assurance of understanding and the knowledge of God's mystery, which is Christ, in whom are hidden all the treasures of wisdom and knowledge. I say this in order that no one may delude you with plausible arguments. For though I am absent in body, yet I am with you in spirit, rejoicing to see your good order and the firmness of your faith in Christ.

LET'S DIVE IN!

Introduction to

Bible Highlighting

Systems

Developing a System

The goal of Bible highlighting is to help us know God more through the study of His Word. It is an effective tool in this regard because it facilitates deeper study as it draws our attention to key words and themes in a text. Essentially, we are dissecting a text rather than casually reading it. It moves us from being passive readers to active readers. This helps us discover deeper truths and meanings that may have gone unnoticed had we not slowed down to highlight.

Here is a sample system of Bible highlighting. Again, this can be modified to best serve the individual. Also, remember that we are not obligated to carry out one particular system throughout the entire Bible. There is flexibility and freedom in the process.

SAMPLE HIGHLIGHTING KEY

Yellow = *Character of God*

Blue = *Redemption*

Green = *Commands to Obey*

Orange = *Nature of Man/Flesh + Sins to Avoid*

Purple = *Book-Specific Key Themes*

Pink = *Verses to Memorize*

Throughout the rest of the book, you will see example passages with the relevant highlighting key applied. These example passages will help you gain a better understanding of elements in Scripture to look for while highlighting.

John 15:1-17

[1]"I am the true vine, and my Father is the gardener. [2]Every branch in me that does not produce fruit he removes, and he prunes every branch that produces fruit so that it will produce more fruit. [3]You are already clean because of the word I have spoken to you. [4]Remain in me, and I in you. Just as a branch is unable to produce fruit by itself unless it remains on the vine, neither can you unless you remain in me. [5]I am the vine; you are the branches. The one who remains in me and I in him produces much fruit, because you can do nothing without me. [6]If anyone does not remain in me, he is thrown aside like a branch and he withers. They gather them, throw them into the fire, and they are burned. [7]If you remain in me and my words remain in you, ask whatever you want and it will be done for you. [8]My Father is glorified by this: that you produce much fruit and prove to be my disciples.

[9]"As the Father has loved me, I have also loved you. Remain in my love. [10]If you keep my commands you will remain in my love, just as I have kept my Father's commands and remain in his love.

[11]"I have told you these things so that my joy may be in you and your joy may be complete.

[12]"This is my command: Love one another as I have loved you. [13]No one has greater love than this: to lay down his life for his friends. [14]You are my friends if you do what I command you. [15]I do not call you servants anymore, because a servant doesn't know what his master is doing. I have called you friends, because I have made known to you everything I have heard from my Father. [16]You did not choose me, but I chose you. I appointed you to go and produce fruit and that your fruit should remain, so that whatever you ask the Father in my name, he will give you.

[17] "This is what I command you: Love one another.

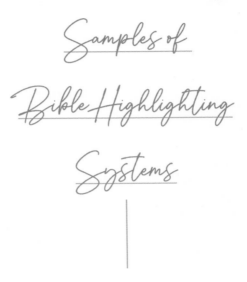

Samples of Bible Highlighting Systems

This section will explore different categories to consider when developing a Bible highlighting system:

ATTRIBUTES OF GOD

MAN'S NATURE / SIN

REDEMPTION

COMMANDS

KEY THEMES

CONTEXT

REPEATED WORDS AND PHRASES

UNION WITH CHRIST /
IDENTITY IN CHRIST

COMPARISONS AND CONTRASTS

LISTS

VERSES TO PRAY

Attributes of God

Reserving a highlighter for the attributes of God is essential for any system. This is because we read the Bible to know God. So as we read, we want to intentionally identify His attributes and character in Scripture. There are verses that explicitly state His nature such as 2 Timothy 2:13, which says, "he remains faithful, for he cannot deny himself;" however, it may not be as direct. His faithfulness is on display throughout Scripture. This applies to His love, goodness, holiness, justice, patience, and grace. He is infinite, self-sufficient, incomprehensible, unchanging, eternal, omniscient, omnipresent, omnipotent, and sovereign. We must train our eyes and minds to identify His nature in Scripture and allow it to change us.

SAMPLE HIGHLIGHTING KEY
Yellow = *Humility*
Pink = *Love*
Blue = *Holiness*

Philippians 2:5-11

[5]Adopt the same attitude as that of Christ Jesus, [6]who, existing in the form of God, did not consider equality with God as something to be exploited. [7]Instead he emptied himself by assuming the form of a servant, taking on the likeness of humanity. And when he had come as a man, [8]he humbled himself by becoming obedient to the point of death — even to death on a cross. [9]For this reason God highly exalted him and gave him the name that is above every name, [10]so that at the name of Jesus every knee will bow — in heaven and on earth and under the earth — [11]and every tongue will confess that Jesus Christ is Lord, to the glory of God the Father.

Man's Nature / Sin

It is helpful to mark the nature of man because it reminds us of the power of the gospel. The more we see our sinful nature and who we are, the more clearly we see the holiness of God. Our sin reminds us of the beauty of the person and work of Christ. We are reminded of our need for Him.

SAMPLE HIGHLIGHTING KEY

Blue = *Redeemed*

Teal = *Unredeemed (man's nature/sin)*

Green = *Commands*

Colossians 3:1-10

[1]So if you have been raised with Christ, seek the things above, where Christ is, seated at the right hand of God. [2]Set your minds on things above, not on earthly things. [3]For you died, and your life is hidden with Christ in God. [4]When Christ, who is your life, appears, then you also will appear with him in glory. [5]Therefore, put to death what belongs to your earthly nature: sexual immorality, impurity, lust, evil desire, and greed, which is idolatry. [6]Because of these, God's wrath is coming upon the disobedient, [7]and you once walked in these things when you were living in them. [8]But now, put away all the following: anger, wrath, malice, slander, and filthy language from your mouth. [9]Do not lie to one another, since you have put off the old self with its practices [10]and have put on the new self. You are being renewed in knowledge according to the image of your Creator.

Redemption

Redemption is a theme woven throughout Scripture. We see it right away in Genesis 3:15 when the gospel is first declared. We also see it in Noah's Ark, the Exodus, and the stories of Ruth and Esther. All of Scripture proclaims the story of redemption, and it all points to Jesus, the One who redeems. Once we train our eyes to see this, we will see it everywhere. There are many types and shadows of Christ throughout the Old Testament (ex. Abraham, Abel, Issac, Moses, David, the Tabernacle, the Temple, etc.) along with passages that explicitly point to Jesus and the ultimate restoration that He will bring (Isaiah 61:1-3). Then there are implications of redemption seen in the New Testament. Ephesians 1:3-10 tells us that believers are chosen in Christ, predestined, adopted, and blessed with every spiritual blessing. We have forgiveness and the riches of His grace. Designating a highlighter to pull out the theme of redemption will help you see the continuity of Scripture and visually show you the overarching story.

SAMPLE HIGHLIGHTING KEY
Blue = *Redeemed*

Exodus 3:7-10

[7]Then the Lord said, "I have observed the misery of my people in Egypt, and have heard them crying out because of their oppressors. I know about their sufferings, [8]and I have come down to rescue them from the power of the Egyptians and to bring them from that land to a good and spacious land, a land flowing with milk and honey — the territory of the Canaanites, Hethites, Amorites, Perizzites, Hivites, and Jebusites. [9]So because the Israelites' cry for help has come to me, and I have also seen the way the Egyptians are oppressing them, [10]therefore, go. I am sending you to Pharaoh so that you may lead my people, the Israelites, out of Egypt."

Genesis 12:1-3

[1]The Lord said to Abram: Go from your land, your relatives, and your father's house to the land that I will show you.

[2]I will make you into a great nation, I will bless you, I will make your name great, and you will be a blessing. [3]I will bless those who bless you, I will curse anyone who treats you with contempt, and all the peoples on earth will be blessed through you.

Isaiah 61:1-3

[1]The Spirit of the Lord God is on me, because the Lord has anointed me to bring good news to the poor. He has sent me to heal the brokenhearted, to proclaim liberty to the captives and freedom to the prisoners;

[2]to proclaim the year of the Lord's favor, and the day of our God's vengeance; to comfort all who mourn,

[3]to provide for those who mourn in Zion; to give them a crown of beauty instead of ashes, festive oil instead of mourning, and splendid clothes instead of despair. And they will be called righteous trees, planted by the Lord to glorify him.

Commands

Scripture is full of commands. Those commands are for our good and His glory. Psalm 19:8 says, "the precepts of the LORD are right, making the heart glad; the command of the LORD is radiant, making the eyes light up." But how do we reconcile the law and grace? It is helpful to remember why we have the law. The law reveals sin as a visible offense to a set standard. Therefore, our need for redemption is undeniable. The law has exposed our sin and cannot redeem us. But by God's grace, we are led to Christ. And it is our union with Christ that leads us to obey His commands. This is a mark of a true believer. Obedience is how we abide in His love (John 15:10), and we should study God's Word with an attitude of faith and obedience.

SAMPLE HIGHLIGHTING KEY

Green = Commands (to do good)

Orange = Commands (to avoid sin)

Romans 12:9-21

⁹Let love be without hypocrisy. Detest evil; cling to what is good. ¹⁰Love one another deeply as brothers and sisters. Take the lead in honoring one another. ¹¹Do not lack diligence in zeal; be fervent in the Spirit; serve the Lord. ¹²Rejoice in hope; be patient in affliction; be persistent in prayer. ¹³Share with the saints in their needs; pursue hospitality. ¹⁴Bless those who persecute you; bless and do not curse. ¹⁵Rejoice with those who rejoice; weep with those who weep. ¹⁶Live in harmony with one another. Do not be proud; instead, associate with the humble. Do not be wise in your own estimation. ¹⁷Do not repay anyone evil for evil. Give careful thought to do what is honorable in everyone's eyes. ¹⁸If possible, as far as it depends on you, live at peace with everyone. ¹⁹Friends, do not avenge yourselves; instead, leave room for God's wrath, because it is written, Vengeance belongs to me; I will repay, says the Lord.

²⁰But

If your enemy is hungry, feed him.
If he is thirsty, give him something to drink.
For in so doing
you will be heaping fiery coals on his head.

²¹Do not be conquered by evil, but conquer evil with good.

Key Themes

Every book in the Bible has key themes woven throughout. These book-specific themes function as secondary themes to the main theme of redemption in the story of Scripture. Every theme serves to more clearly flesh out who God is and what His plan of redemption is for His people. Thus, highlighting these key themes will help us have a fuller understanding of the gospel.

SAMPLE HIGHLIGHTING KEY

Pink = *Rejoice, Adore, Worship*

Yellow = *Promise of God*

Green = *Command*

Philippians 4:4-9

[4]Rejoice in the Lord always. I will say it again: Rejoice! [5]Let your graciousness be known to everyone. The Lord is near. [6]Don't worry about anything, but in everything, through prayer and petition with thanksgiving, present your requests to God. [7]And the peace of God, which surpasses all understanding, will guard your hearts and minds in Christ Jesus. [8]Finally brothers and sisters, whatever is true, whatever is honorable, whatever is just, whatever is pure, whatever is lovely, whatever is commendable—if there is any moral excellence and if there is anything praiseworthy—dwell on these things. [9]Do what you have learned and received and heard from me, and seen in me, and the God of peace will be with you.

Context

It is of utmost importance to study the Bible in context. This takes work because we naturally approach Scripture with personal biases that are shaped by our own culture and history. It takes work to study a passage with the intent of understanding the original meaning. The goal is to see what the author of a passage meant for his original audience. We can begin this process by highlighting parts of the text that help us understand the author and his background, the time period it was written, the intended audience, the genre of the text, and the purpose it was written. A helpful resource to answer these historical questions (time written, etc.) is the ESV Study Bible.

SAMPLE HIGHLIGHTING KEY

Yellow = *Who wrote it?*

Orange = *To whom was it written?*

Blue = *Where is this taking place?*

Green = *When was this written?*

Purple = *Why was this written?*

(approx. 50 AD)

Asia Minor / Modern day Turkey

Galatians 1:1-9

[1]Paul, an apostle—not from men or by man, but by Jesus Christ and God the Father who raised him from the dead— [2]and all the brothers who are with me: To the churches of Galatia. [3]Grace to you and peace from God the Father and our Lord Jesus Christ, [4]who gave himself for our sins to rescue us from this present evil age, according to the will of our God and Father. [5]To him be the glory forever and ever. Amen.

[6]I am amazed that you are so quickly turning away from him who called you by the grace of Christ and are turning to a different gospel— [7]not that there is another gospel, but there are some who are troubling you and want to distort the gospel of Christ. [8]But even if we or an angel from heaven should preach to you a gospel contrary to what we have preached to you, a curse be on him! [9]As we have said before, I now say again: If anyone is preaching to you a gospel contrary to what you received, a curse be on him!

Repeated Words and Phrases

Repetition in Scripture always conveys a sense of importance. So whenever a word or a group of words are repeated in a passage, we should take note and see how these key words and phrases reveal the author's intent for the passage. You can reserve a highlighter to mark the different keywords in different books of the Bible. If you want to take it a step further, you can dig deeper into those repeated words in the Hebrew and Greek. You may find that the same English word may have actually been different words in the original language, and there is much to learn from the nuances of translations. Helpful resources include: LOGOS, blueletterbible.org, or concordances.

SAMPLE HIGHLIGHTING KEY

Yellow = *Command to be Fruitful/Multiply*

Blue = *God*

Green = *Covenant/Sign of the Covenant*

Purple = *Creatures*

Pink = *Covenant Establishment*

Teal = *Noah and His Family/Humanity*

Genesis 9:1-17

¹God blessed Noah and his sons and said to them, "Be fruitful and multiply and fill the earth. ²The fear and terror of you will be in every living creature on the earth, every bird of the sky, every creature that crawls on the ground, and all the fish of the sea. They are placed under your authority. ³Every creature that lives and moves will be food for you; as I gave the green plants, I have given you everything. ⁴However, you must not eat meat with its lifeblood in it. ⁵And I will require a penalty for your lifeblood; I will require it from any animal and from any human; if someone murders a fellow human, I will require that person's life.

⁶Whoever sheds human blood,
by humans his blood will be shed,
for God made humans in his image.

⁷But you, be fruitful and multiply; spread out over the earth and multiply on it." ⁸Then God said to Noah and his sons with him, ⁹"Understand that I am establishing my covenant with you and your descendants after you, ¹⁰and with every living creature that is with you—birds, livestock, and all wildlife of the earth that are with you—all the animals of the earth that came out of the ark. ¹¹I establish my covenant with you that never again will every creature be wiped out by floodwaters; there will never again be a flood to destroy the earth." ¹²And God said, "This is the sign of the covenant I am making between me and you and every living creature with you, a covenant for all future generations: ¹³I have placed my bow in the clouds, and it will be a sign of the covenant between me and the earth. ¹⁴Whenever I form clouds over the earth and the bow appears in the clouds, ¹⁵I will remember my covenant between me and you and all the living creatures: water will never again become a flood to destroy every creature. ¹⁶The bow will be in the clouds, and I will look at it and remember the permanent covenant between God and all the living creatures on earth." ¹⁷God said to Noah, "This is the sign of the covenant that I have established between me and every creature on earth."

Union with Christ and Identity in Christ

The Apostle Paul refers to the union between believers and the Lord Jesus over 160 times. As we study God's Word and get to know who He is, we will learn who we are in Him. This doctrine of union with Christ speaks to our identity, and our new identity in Christ is an implication of our redemption. We are "God's Children" (1 John 3:1). Likewise, we are the body of Christ (1 Corinthians 12:27). Highlighting these truths will help us have a better grasp of who we are individually and corporately.

SAMPLE HIGHLIGHTING KEY

Yellow = *God*

Blue = *Redeemed Man*

Pink = *Union with Christ*

Green = *Commands*

John 15:1-8

[1]I am the true vine, and my Father is the gardener. [2]Every branch in me that does not produce fruit he removes, and he prunes every branch that produces fruit so that it will produce more fruit. [3]You are already clean because of the word I have spoken to you. [4]Remain in me, and I in you. Just as a branch is unable to produce fruit by itself unless it remains on the vine, neither can you unless you remain in me. [5]I am the vine; you are the branches. The one who remains in me and I in him produces much fruit, because you can do nothing without me. [6]If anyone does not remain in me, he is thrown aside like a branch and he withers. They gather them, throw them into the fire, and they are burned. [7]If you remain in me and my words remain in you, ask whatever you want and it will be done for you. [8]My Father is glorified by this: that you produce much fruit and prove to be my disciples.

Comparisons and Contrasts

Metaphors are commonly used throughout Scripture as a tool for comparison. A metaphor is a comparison between two or more things using figurative language, and it is a helpful literary tool because it simplifies complex ideas. Metaphors about God are common in Scripture, and they aid our understanding of His character (ex. Deuteronomy 32:4 refers to God as "the Rock"). We are also better able to understand who we are in light of who God is through the use of metaphors (ex. John 15:5). Contrasts are also helpful for us to grasp the truth, and they can be identified in Scripture with transition words like "but," "however," and "rather." For example, in Ephesians 4:28-32, we see a string of contrasts: stealing verses laboring and doing honest work; corrupt talk verses words that build others up; bitterness, wrath, anger, and slander verses kindness, tenderheartedness, and forgiveness. Many stark contrasts between walking in the flesh and walking in the Spirit are noted throughout the Apostle Paul's epistles. Highlighting these contrasts helps us clearly see the transforming work of the gospel.

SAMPLE HIGHLIGHTING KEY

Yellow = *New Man*

Teal = *Old Man*

Romans 6:1-14

[1]What should we say then? Should we continue in sin so that grace may multiply? [2]Absolutely not! How can we who died to sin still live in it? [3]Or are you unaware that all of us who were baptized into Christ Jesus were baptized into his death? [4]Therefore we were buried with him by baptism into death, in order that, just as Christ was raised from the dead by the glory of the Father, so we too may walk in newness of life. [5]For if we have been united with him in the likeness of his death, we will certainly also be in the likeness of his resurrection. [6]For we know that our old self was crucified with him so that the body ruled by sin might be rendered powerless so that we may no longer be enslaved to sin, [7]since a person who has died is freed from sin. [8]Now if we died with Christ, we believe that we will also live with him, [9]because we know that Christ, having been raised from the dead, will not die again. Death no longer rules over him. [10]For the death he died, he died to sin once for all time; but the life he lives, he lives to God. [11]So, you too consider yourselves dead to sin and alive to God in Christ Jesus. [12]Therefore do not let sin reign in your mortal body, so that you obey its desires. [13]And do not offer any parts of it to sin as weapons for unrighteousness. But as those who are alive from the dead, offer yourselves to God, and all the parts of yourselves to God as weapons for righteousness. [14]For sin will not rule over you, because you are not under the law but under grace.

Lists

There are many lists in Scripture. These lists often require us to slow down in our reading. Highlighting, marking these with numbers, or writing these in the margin of your Bible will help you have a better understanding of the passage.

Here are some suggested passages to help you develop a system for identifying lists in Scripture:

Proverbs 6:6–19

1 Corinthians 13:4–7

Galatians 2:19–21

Galatians 5:22–23

Ephesians 4:31–32

Colossians 3:5–10

James 4:7–11

You might prefer to study lists in Scripture by printing out a double-spaced copy of the passage to allow more space for annotating.

1 Peter 5:6-9

①⁶Humble yourselves, therefore, under the mighty hand of God, so that he may exalt you at the proper time, ②⁷casting all your cares on him, because he cares about you. ⁸Be sober-minded, ③④ be alert. Your adversary the devil is prowling around like a roaring lion, looking for anyone he can devour. ⑤⁹Resist him, firm in the faith, knowing that the same kind of sufferings are being experienced by your fellow believers throughout the world.

1. be humble
2. give God your worry/concern
3/4. be watchful/discreet
5. resist the devil

Verses to Pray

Prayer is personal, but this does not mean we are required to only use our own words every time we pray. We can use Scripture to guide our prayers. There are many passages that we can pray directly back to the Lord. If praying Scripture is new to you, start in the book of Psalms. The Psalms were designed to be sung or prayed back to God. You can use an entire psalm directly as a prayer, like Psalm 51.

SAMPLE HIGHLIGHTING KEY

Pink = *Verses to Turn into Prayers*

Ephesians 1:15–19

[15]This is why, since I heard about your faith in the Lord Jesus and your love for all the saints, [16]I never stop giving thanks for you as I remember you in my prayers. [17]I pray that the God of our Lord Jesus Christ, the glorious Father, would give you the Spirit of wisdom and revelation in the knowledge of him. [18]I pray that the eyes of your heart may be enlightened so that you may know what is the hope of his calling, what is the wealth of his glorious inheritance in the saints, [19]and what is the immeasurable greatness of his power toward us who believe, according to the mighty working of his strength.

Psalm 119:9-18

[9] How can a young man keep his way pure?
By keeping your word.

[10] I have sought you with all my heart;
don't let me wander from your commands.

[11] I have treasured your word in my heart
so that I may not sin against you.

[12] Lord, may you be blessed;
teach me your statutes.

[13] With my lips I proclaim
all the judgments from your mouth.

[14] I rejoice in the way revealed by your decrees
as much as in all riches.

[15] I will meditate on your precepts
and think about your ways.

[16] I will delight in your statutes;
I will not forget your word.

[17] Deal generously with your servant
so that I might live;
then I will keep your word.

[18] Open my eyes so that I may contemplate
wondrous things from your instruction.

Other Categories

Here are other categories to consider. These are broader categories that you can keep in mind as you read through the entire Bible. Examples are not provided because this approach may involve noting one or two verses in entire books of the Bible. However, intentionally marking even these few threads can help you see the cohesive nature of the Word of God and marvel how it truly is one, grand narrative.

JESUS IN THE OLD TESTAMENT

Jesus is the main character of Scripture, both the Old and New Testaments. The Old Testament contains many prophecies of Jesus. Some are very obvious and familiar, while others will require a more intentional study that requires careful digging. There are also many types and shadows of Christ. For example, Adam was a type of Christ in that he represented humanity (Romans 5:12-21). Other types include Abel, Seth, Isaac, Moses, David, and more. Identifying these helps us see the continuity of the story of redemption.

BIBLICAL THEOLOGY APPROACH

This approach traces a particular theme in the story of Scripture from creation to consummation. There are many significant themes woven throughout Scripture: covenants, kingdom, sacrifice, temple, feasts, and more. Perhaps one year you focus on one particular theme as you read through the Bible and designate a highlighter for that theme.

STORY OF SCRIPTURE

The metanarrative of Scripture is best understood through four plot movements: creation, fall, redemption, and restoration. These movements encapsulate the central message of the whole Bible. It may be helpful to designate one highlighter color for each plot movement and see the unfolding of this grand story of redemption throughout the pages of God's Word.

MEANINGFUL VERSES OR THEMES

There are seasons in life when specific themes or concepts are more meaningful to you. You can use a highlighter color to identify that theme or concept throughout the Bible. Or maybe the Lord uses a particular passage of Scripture to encourage you in a difficult season of life—you can mark these verses and even add a date and/or description in the margins of your Bible to document His faithfulness and encouragement to you.

VERSES TO MEMORIZE

There may be specific verses you want to commit to memory. These verses may not fall under the same topic, but the specific highlighter color may remind you of your desire to memorize that particular verse.

will abide in the Son and in the Father. ²⁵ And this is the promise that he made

to us[1]—eternal life.

²⁶ I write these things to you about those who are trying to deceive you. ²⁷ But

the anointing that you received from him abides in you, and you have no need

that anyone should teach you. But as his anointing teaches you about everything,

and is true, and is no lie—just as it has taught you, abide in him.

Children of God

²⁸ And now, little children, abide in him, so that when he appears we may

have confidence and not shrink from him in shame at his coming. ²⁹ If you know

that he is righteous, you may be sure that everyone who practices righteousness

what is righteousness?

has been born of him.

1. consistent w/ the nature of christ v.29

3 See what kind of love the Father has given to us, that we should be called

2. lovingly saved by God v. 1 3. meaningfully named by God v. 1

children of God; and so we are. The reason why the world does not know us is

that it did not know him. ² Beloved, we are God's children now, and what we will

be has not yet appeared; but we know that when he appears[2] we shall be like him,

because we shall see him as he is. ³ And everyone who thus hopes in him purifies

himself as he is pure.

as He is, so are His followers—

⁴ Everyone who makes a practice of sinning also practices lawlessness; sin is

^{1 Some manuscripts you} ^{2 Or when it appears}

There are many themes that can be traced in Scripture. Though each book has its own prominent themes, many of these themes can be found throughout Scripture. It's helpful to consider these individual themes and see how they tie into the overall narrative of redemption woven throughout the Bible.

You can assign one highlighter color to each theme. As you work through an annual Bible reading plan, choose one or two to keep in mind as you read.

HERE ARE SOME THEMES TO CONSIDER:

Blessing & Curse

Clean & Unclean

Clothing

Covenants & Promises

Creation & Recreation

Deliverance

Evangelism

Exodus & Exile

Faith

Fellowship Feasts

Future Hope

Garden & Wilderness

Glory

God's Dwelling Place

God & His Character

Holiness

Immanuel

Joy

King & Kingdom

Lament

Light & Darkness

Love

Marriage

Obedience

Offspring & Seed

The People of God

Priesthood

Promised Land

Redemption & Grace

Sacrifice

Sin & Judgment

Suffering & Trials

Tabernacle & Temple

Work & Rest

Worship

Other Considerations

CROSS REFERENCES

A cross reference is a verse in Scripture that corresponds to another verse in Scripture. Bibles typically have these references noted in the margins or at the bottom of the page. If not, they can be found at different online resources or in commentaries. A free option is www.biblegateway.com. Cross references can be helpful in personal Bible study because they guide the interpretation of Scripture. They show connections between texts. Before seeking insight from commentaries on a passage, it is highly recommended that you look up cross references and allow that to aid you in your interpretation of the passage at hand.

WORD STUDIES

Word studies can greatly expand your understanding on biblical concepts. The Bible was originally written in three different languages: Hebrew, Aramaic, and Greek. Sometimes one word in the original language can be translated into many different English words or one English word can be used in translation of various Greek or Hebrew words. Therefore, it is sometimes beneficial to look up those words to gain a deeper understanding of the text.

There are many different types of transition words. These different transition words or phrases are useful because they show the relationship between different passages, and they provide a sense of cohesion in the author's writing. The meaning of the text is more fully, clearly, and accurately seen because of these transition words, so they are important to note.

They can be used to show:

1. Emphasis (*importantly, absolutely, in particular, it should be noted, etc.*)

2. Addition (*furthermore, also, to, along with, moreover, but also, etc.*)

3. Contrast (*nevertheless, despite, in contrast to, while, where as, even so, etc.*)

4. Order (*first or firstly, before, subsequently, above all, following, first and foremost, etc.*)

5. Result (*therefore, thus, hence, for this reason, due to, etc.*)

6. Illustration (*for example, such as, including, namely, like, etc.*)

7. Comparison (*similarly, likewise, just as, in the same way, etc.*)

8. Summary (*in conclusion, altogether, etc.*)

9. Reason (*because of, with this in mind, in fact, in order to, due to, etc.*)

10. Condition (*if, in case, unless, etc.*)

11. Concession (*admittedly, even so, although, even though, however, etc.*)

Conclusion

We need the Lord's help in understanding His Word. He is the One who can illume our minds as we read His Word, and the Spirit transforms us by the renewal of our minds (Romans 12:2). Through prayer, our time in the Word becomes supernatural and transformative with enduring spiritual fruit. Pray through Psalm 119. Below are some verses that you could pray verbatim before beginning your time in God's Word.

from Psalm 119

[18]*Open my eyes so that I may contemplate*
wonderous things from your instruction.

[27]*Help me understand the meaning of your precepts*
so that I can meditate on your wonders.

[29]*Keep me from the way of deceit*
and graciously give me your instruction.

[33]*Teach me, Lord, the meaning of your statutes,*
and I will always keep them.

[34]*Help me understand your instruction, and I will*
obey it and follow it with my whole heart.

[35]*Help me stay on the path of your commands,*
for I take pleasure in it.

[36]*Turn my heart to your decrees*
and not to dishonest profit.

[37]*Turn my eyes from looking at what is worthless;*
give me life in your ways.